DATE DUE	

BOA CONSTRICTORS

THE SNAKE DISCOVERY LIBRARY

Sherie Bargar   Linda Johnson

Photographer/Consultant: George Van Horn

Rourke Enterprises, Inc.
Vero Beach, Florida 32964

Library of Congress Cataloging in Publication Data

Bargar, Sherie, 1944-
  Discover Boa constrictors.

  (Snake discovery library)
  Summary: Discusses the natural habitats, physical
characteristics, life cycle, and behavior of these
non-poisonous snakes.
  Includes index.
  1. Boidae—Juvenile literature.   2. Boa constrictor—
Juvenile literature. [1. Boa constrictor.   2. Snakes]
I. Johnson, Linda, 1947-   . II. Van Horn,
George, ill.   III. Title.   IV. Series: Bargar,
Sherie, 1944-   . Snake discovery library.
QL666.063B37   1986   597.96   86-15576
ISBN 0-86592-959-9

Title Photo:
Cook's Tree
Boa coo

TABLE OF CONTENTS

BOA CONSTRICTORS

All species of boas are non-poisonous snakes in the *Boidae* family. Powerful, gripping jaws and long, **penetrating** teeth combined with a strong muscular body are a source of many **myths** about this giant among snakes. In spite of the awesome **myths**, the boa constrictor has become very popular in the pet industry.

WHERE THEY LIVE

The grasslands and tropical forests from Mexico to Argentina are the homes of the Boa family. Each species of boa has special needs. The Common Boa Constrictor is a ground dweller while the Anaconda spends most of its time in water. The Emerald Tree Boa is a rain forest snake living in the forest **canopy**.

Rainbow Boa
Epicrates cencl

HOW THEY LOOK

The Common Boa Constrictor has a tan body with dark chocolate bands changing to red markings on a white tail. Other boas are red, green, brown, or black with patterns or bands. The long, heavy body of the Boa Constrictor may grow to 15 feet.

mmon Boa Constrictor

THEIR SENSES

The Boa Constrictor relies on the sense of smell in locating **prey**. It flicks its tongue out and brings in particles from the surrounding area. The Jacobson's organ in the roof of its mouth **analyzes** the particles to learn what is nearby. At close range, the Boa Constrictor identifies size and location of **prey** by sight. The Boa Constrictor does not have heat receptor pits, but other species do. The Emerald Tree Boa has highly developed heat receptor pits.

ᴊerald Tree Boa
Corallus canina

THE HEAD AND MOUTH

Boa Constrictors have triangular shaped heads with very strong jaws. They do not have any fangs, but long teeth that are used to **penetrate** through feathers of birds and the skins of animals. The windpipe extends from the throat to the front of the mouth. It lets the snake breathe while swallowing **prey**. After its **prey** has been killed, the jaws stretch like a rubber band to swallow the animals whole.

BABY BOA CONSTRICTORS

In mid to late summer mother boa constrictors have as many as 50 babies. They are about 2 feet long and weigh about 4 to 5 ounces. At birth baby boas can kill and swallow mice. Within one year, a baby boa may grow to a length of 8 feet and weigh 40 pounds.

Juvenile Emerald Tree E

PREY

Boas eat large **prey** including birds, lizards, rodents, fish, and wild pigs. Boas strike quickly at the **prey's** head, then wrap or coil around the **prey**. The **prey** is not crushed only held in place firmly. Each time the **prey** breathes out, the coils of the boa tighten around its chest. This stops the **prey** from being able to breathe and it **suffocates**. This method of killing is known as constriction.

mmon Boa Constrictor
Boa constrictor

THEIR DEFENSE

The adult Boa Constrictor has few natural enemies because of its large size. When an enemy comes too close to a boa, it relies mainly on **camouflage** for its defense. Although some boas are gentle when captured, others will hiss and bite.

Cook's Tree E
Boa coo

BOA CONSTRICTORS AND PEOPLE

For many years Boa Constrictors have been popular pets. They often thrive in captivity, but should always be regarded as wild animals. The oldest living Boa Constrictor is kept in the London Zoo and is over 40 years old.

GLOSSARY

analyze (AN a lyze) analyzes — To find out what something is.

camouflage (CAM ou flage) — The color of an animal's skin matches the ground around it.

canopy (CAN o py) — The top layer of the trees which cover the forest.

myth (MYTH) myths — An idea that comes from tall tales rather than facts.

penetrate (PEN e trate) penetrating — To enter.

prey (PREY) — An animal hunted or killed by another animal for food.

suffocate (SUF fo cate) suffocates — To kill by not allowing an animal to breathe.

INDEX